DOLL'S CLOTHES
in Double Knitting

This book is a revised edition of old Paragon knitting book N56 "Doll's Clothes in Double Knitting", originally published by Paragon Art Needlecraft Pty Ltd, Sydney, NSW. Craft Moods is now the copyright owner and publisher for all Paragon publications.

Edited by: Vicki Moodie.

Copyright: Ray and Vicki Moodie   2000

Revised: October 2006

ISBN 978-1-876373-67-2

Published by

CRAFT MOODS
PO Box 35
Glass House Mtns Qld. 4518
Australia

Tel (07) 53756266

www.craftmoods.com.au

Printed by   Print Approach
10 Frawley Ave
NARANGBA QLD 4504

Tel (07) 38882488

CONTENTS

ABBREVIATIONS

K	knit
P	purl
psso	pass slip stitch over
st(s)	stitch(es)
tog	together
yfwd	yarn forward

garter st: all rows knit.

stocking st: knit row followed by a purl row.

moss st: (K1, P1) alternatively, beginning each row with the same stitch that ends the previous row.

GENERAL INSTRUCTIONS

The patterns in this book are knitted with 8ply yarn using 3.75mm knitting needles to give a TENSION of 22sts to 10cm. A 3mm crochet hook is also used for edging.

K- (1, 4), means there are 3 sizes, knit none for the first size, K1 for the second size and K4 for the third size.

BABY DOLL OUTFIT

To fit doll sizes:
30 (**35,** 40, **51**)cm in height

Chest: 25.5 (**29.5,** 33, **40.5**)cm

MATERIALS:
Complete Set:
10 (**14,** 14, **18**) 25g balls of 8ply yarn

Vest:
1 (**1,** 1, **3**) 25g balls of 8ply yarn

Pilchers:
1 (**1,** 1, **1**) 25g balls of 8ply yarn
30cm of elastic

Dress and Bootees:
4 (**5,** 5, **6**) 25g balls of 8ply yarn
1.35m of 7mm wide ribbon
2 small buttons

Short Jacket:
1 (**3,** 3, **4**) 25g balls of 8ply yarn
1 small button for neck

Matinee Jacket:
(patterned skirt)
3 (**4,** 4, **5**) 25g balls
of 8ply yarn;
70cm of 7mm wide
ribbon

Bonnet:
1 (**1,** 1, **3**) 25g balls
of 8ply yarn;
70cm of 12mm wide
ribbon

VEST

Cast on 28 (**32**, 36, **44**)sts and work in (K2, P2) rib for 8 (**9.5**, 11, **14**)cm.

Shape neck:
Rib 8 (**10**, 10, **12**)sts, cast off 12 (**12**, 16, **20**)sts, rib 8 (**10**, 10, **12**)sts. (16, **20**, 20, **24**sts)
Rib 5 (**5**, 5, **7.5**)cm on the first group of sts, ending at inside edge. Break off yarn.

Rejoin yarn to the second group of sts and work 5 (**5**, 5, **7.5**)cm, ending at the inside edge.

Cast on 12 (**12**, 16, **20**)sts, and work across the remaining group of sts. (28, **32**, 36, **44**sts)
Continue in rib for 9.5 (**11.5**, 12, **15**)cm. Cast off in rib.

Make up:
Fold over the work so that the cast-off edge is level with the cast-on edge. Stitch each side seam, leaving sufficient room at the top for the armholes.

PILCHERS

Cast on 28 (**32**, 36, **40**)sts and work 4 rows in stocking st.
Row 5. (Right side) Purl.
Continue in stocking st (beginning with a purl row) until work measures 5.5 (**6**, 6.5, **7**) cm from row 5.

Shape legs:
K2 tog at each end of every row until 6 (**6**, 6, **10**)sts remain.
Work on these sts for 3 (**5**, 5, **7**) rows.
Now increase one st at each end of every row until there are 28 (**32**, 36, **40**)sts on the needle.

Work 5.5 (**6**, 6.5, **7**)cm in stocking stitch.
Work a row of purl on right side and then work 4 more rows of stocking stitch beginning with a purl row. Cast off.

Make up:
Join side seams. Fold over a hem to wrong side on purl row and stitch. Thread elastic through hem.

DRESS

DRESS FRONT

Cast on 44 (**50**, 56, **60**)sts and make a picot hem as follows:
Work 2 rows in stocking st.

Row 3. K1, * yfwd, K2 tog; repeat from * to last st, K1.
Work 3 more rows in stocking st, beginning with a purl row.

Row 7. K1, * K2 tog, yfwd; repeat from * to last st, K1.
Row 8. K1, purl to last st, K1.
Row 9. K1, * yfwd, K2 tog; repeat from * to last st, K1.
Row 10. K1, purl to last st, K1.

Repeat last 4 rows until the work measures 11.5 (**12.5**, 14, **16**)cm from row of holes for picot edge.

Next row (for 30, 35 and 40cm sizes). Decrease as follows, with right side facing: * K1, K2 tog; repeat from * to last 2sts, K2. (30, 34, 38sts)

Next row (for 51cm size). Decrease as follows, with right side facing: K3, * K2 tog, K2; repeat from * to last 5sts, K2 tog, K3. (46sts)

All sizes
Next row. Knit.
Next row. (Ribbon holes) * K1, yfwd, K2 tog; repeat from * to end of row / **(to last st, K1)** / (to last 2sts, K2) / **(to last st, K1)**.
Next row. Knit.
Work 4 rows in stocking st.

Raglan shaping:
Cast off 3 (**3**, 3, **5**)sts at the beginning of each of the next 2 rows.
(24, **28**, 32, **36sts**)

Row 3. K1, slip 1, K1, psso, knit to last 3sts, K2 tog, K1.
(22, **26**, 30, **34sts**)
Row 4. K1, purl to last st, K1.
Repeat rows 3 and 4 until 16 (**16**, 18, **22**)sts remain.
Next row. Purl.
Next row. K1, slip 1, K1, psso, K3, cast off 4 (**4**, 6, **10**)sts, K3, K2 tog, K1. (10sts)

Next row. Purl.
Next row. (K2 tog) twice, K1.
Next row. K1, P2 tog.
Next row. K2.
Next row. P2 tog. Fasten off.

Rejoin yarn to remaining sts at the neck edge.
Next row. Purl.
Next row. K1, slip 1, K1, psso, K2 tog.
Next row. P2 tog, K1.
Next row. K2.
Next row. P2 tog. Fasten off.

DRESS BACK
Work as given for the front until the holes for ribbon and waist band are completed.

Divide for back:
K15 (**17**, 19, **23**)sts, turn, cast on 2sts. (17, **19**, 21, **25sts**)
Next row. K3, purl to last st, K1.
Work 2 rows in stocking st keeping the 3 centre edge sts in garter st.

Raglan shaping:
Cast off 3 (**3**, 3, **5**)sts, knit to end of row. (14, **16**, 18, **20sts**)
Row 2. K3, purl to last st, K1.
Row 3. K1, slip 1, psso, knit to end of row. (13, **15**, 17, **19sts**)
Repeat last 2 rows until 11 (**13**, 15, **17**)sts remain, ending with row 2.
Next row. K1, slip 1, K1, psso, knit to last 2sts, yfwd, K2 tog.
(buttonhole made)

Continue with raglan, decrease until 8 (**9**, 10, **12**)sts remain, making another buttonhole at the end of this row.
Repeat rows 2 and 3 twice more. (6, **7**, 8, **10sts**) Cast off.

Join yarn to inside edge of second side and cast on 2sts, knit to end.
Next row. Purl to last 3sts, K3.
Next row. Knit.

Raglan shaping:
Cast off 3 (**3**, 3, **5**)sts, purl to last 3sts, K3.
Continue as for first side, omitting button holes but knitting 2sts tog inside the end st at armhole edge of the decrease rows, until 6 (**7**, 8, **10**)sts remain. Cast off.

DRESS SLEEVES (make 2)
Cast on 26 (**28**, 30, **34**)sts and work the first 6 rows of dress (for the hem), then continue in stocking st for 4 (**4**, 6, **8**) rows.

Shape raglan as for dress, decrease until 4sts remain. Cast off.

Make up:
Stitch sleeves into position. Sew on buttons to correspond with button holes. Fold up hems to rows of holes onto wrong side and sew. Thread 75cm of ribbon through the holes at waist. Work a row of double crochet around neck.

SHORT JACKET (See page 3)

SHORT JACKET BACK
Cast on 32 (**36,** 40, **48**)sts and work the first 6 rows of dress for the hem, then work 4 (**4,** 6, **10**) rows in stocking st.

Raglan shaping:
Work as for front of dress until 10 (**12,** 14, **18**)sts remain. Cast off.

SHORT JACKET RIGHT FRONT
Cast on 12 (**14,**16, **20**)sts and work the first 6 rows of dress for the hem, then work 3 (**3,** 5, **9**) rows in stocking st.

Raglan shaping (wrong side facing):
Cast off 3 (**3,** 3, **5**)sts, purl to end.
Next row. Knit to last 3sts, K2 tog, K1.
Next row. Purl.
Repeat these 2 rows until 2 (**4,** 6, **8**)sts remain.
Next row. Purl.

Shape neck:
30cm Size only: Cast off 1 stitch.
Next Row. Purl. Fasten off.

35cm Size only: Cast off 1 stitch, knit to end. (3sts)
Next Row. Purl.
Next Row. K2 tog, K1. (2sts)
Next Row. P2 tog. Fasten off.

40cm Size only: Cast off 2sts, K2 tog, K1. (3sts)
Next Row. Purl.
Next Row. K2 tog, K1. (2sts)
Next Row. P2 tog. Fasten off.

51cm Size only: Cast off 3sts, K1, K2 tog, K1. (4sts)
Next Row. Purl.
Next Row. K1, K2 tog, K1. (3sts)
Next Row. P2 tog, P1. Fasten off.

SHORT JACKET LEFT FRONT
Work as given for right front reversing all shapings, but work an extra row before beginning the raglan shaping (right side facing) and working K1, slip 1, K1, psso, instead of K2 tog.

SHORT JACKET SLEEVES
(make 2)
Cast on 16 (**18,** 20, **24**)sts and work the first 6 rows of dress for hem.

Working in stocking st, increase one st at each end of the 3rd row and every following 3rd (**3rd**, 4th, **4th**) row until there are 26 (**28,** 30, **34**)sts on the needle.

Work until the sleeve measures 6.5 (**7,** 7.5, **10**)cm from the holes for picot hem, ending with a purl row.

Raglan shaping:
Work as given for the dress until 4 (**4,** 6, **6**)sts remain. Cast off.

Make up:

Join raglan seams, side and sleeve seams. Fold hems up along row of holes at base of jacket and sleeves and sew on the wrong side.

BORDER

With right side facing, join in yarn and pick up and knit 12 (**13,** 14, **16**)sts up right front to make picot border as follows:

Next row. Purl.

Next row. K1, * yfwd, K2 tog; repeat from * to last st, K1.

Work 3 rows in stocking st.

Cast off.

With right side facing, join in yarn at neck of left front and work to correspond.

Fold hems on row of holes to wrong side and sew as before.

Using crochet hook work a row of double crochet around neck, making a small chain loop at top of right hand side for buttonhole.

MATINEE JACKET

MATINEE JACKET BACK

Cast on 44 (**50,** 56, **60**)sts and work as for front of dress until work measures 6.5 (**7,** 8.5, **9.5**)cm from row of holes for picot edge, ending with the right side facing when working next row. Still continue as for front of dress, but work raglan decreases until 10 (**12,** 14, **18**)sts remain. Cast off.

MATINEE JACKET LEFT FRONT

Cast on 24 (**28,** 30, **32**)sts.
Row 1. Knit.
Row 2. K3, purl to end.
Row 3. K1, * yfwd, K2 tog; repeat from * to last 3sts, K3.
Row 4. K3, purl to last st, K1.
Row 5. Knit.
Row 6. K3, purl to last st, K1.
Row 7. K1, * K2 tog, yfwd; repeat from * to last 3sts, K3.
Row 8. K3, purl to last st, K1.
Row 9. K1, * yfwd, K2 tog; repeat from * to last 3sts, K3.
Row 10. K3, purl to last st, K1.

Repeat last 4 rows until work measures 6.5 (**7,** 8.5, **9.5**)cm from row of holes for picot edge, ending with row 10.

Next row for 30cm size:
K1, * K2 tog, K4; repeat from * to last 5sts, K2 tog, K3. (20sts)

Next row for 35cm size:
K1, * K2 tog, K2; repeat from * to last 3sts, K3. (22sts)
Next row for 40cm size:
K1, * K2 tog, K3; repeat from * to last 4sts, K2 tog, K2. (24sts)
Next row for 51cm size:
K1, * K2 tog, K3; repeat from * to last 6sts, K2 tog, K4. (26sts)

All sizes:
Next row. Knit.
Next row. (Ribbon holes) * K1, yfwd, K2 tog; repeat from * to last 2 (**1,** -, **2**)sts and knit these.
Next row. Knit.
Beginning with a knit row, work 2 rows in stocking st, keeping the 3sts for front border in garter st.
Next row. Knit to the last 5sts, K2 tog, K3.
Next row. K3, purl to last st, K1.
Next row. Cast off 3 (**3,** 3, **5**)sts, knit to last 3sts, K3.
Next row. K3, purl to last st, K1.
Next row. K1, slip 1, K1, psso, knit to last 5sts, K2 tog, K3.
Next row. K3, purl to last st, K1.
Next row. K1, slip 1, K1, psso, knit to end of row.
Next row. K3, purl to the last st, K1.
Repeat the last 4 rows until 5 (**6,** 6, **6**)sts remain.
Next row. K3, P1 (**2,** 2, **2**), K1.
Next row. K- (**1,** 1, **1**), K2 tog, K3. (4, **5,** 5, **5sts**)
Next row. K2 tog, K2 (**3,** 3, **3**).

(Sizes 35cm, 40cm and 51cm only):
K2, K2 tog. (3sts)
All sizes: Work 16 (**18**, 20, **24**) rows in garter st on remaining 3sts. Cast off.

MATINEE JACKET RIGHT FRONT

Work as given for left front, but working garter st border at opposite end of row and reversing all shapings. Cast off.

SLEEVES (make 2)

Cast on 16 (**18**, 20, **24**)sts and work as for first 6 rows of dress.
Working in stocking st, increase one st at each end of the 3rd row and every following 3rd (**3rd**, 4th, **4th**) row until there are 26 (**28**, 30, **34**)sts on the needle.
Continue without shaping until the sleeve measures 6.5 (**7**, 7.5, **10**)cm from the holes for picot hem.

Raglan shaping:
Work as given for the dress until 4 (**4**, 6, **6**)sts remain. Cast off.

Make up:
Join raglan seams and side / sleeve seams. Join the two pieces of front band together and stitch into place around the back of the neck. Thread ribbon through holes at waist. Fold hems up along row of holes at base of jacket and sleeves and sew on wrong side.

BONNET

Cast on 32 (**36**, 40, **52**)sts.
Work 4 rows in stocking st.
Row 5. K1, * yfwd, K2 tog; repeat from * to the last st, K1.
Work 5 rows in stocking st.
Next work in pattern as for front of dress but keep 3sts in garter stitch at each end of rows until work measures 5 (**6.5**, 6.5, **8.5**)cm from row of holes for picot edge.
Keeping 3sts in garter st, work in stocking stitch for 2.5 (**2.5**, 4, **5**)cm.

Decrease for crown:
Row 1. * K2 tog, K2; repeat from * to end. (24, **27**, 30, **39sts**)

Row 2 and every alternate row. Purl.
Row 3. * K1, K2 tog; repeat from * to end. (16, **18**, 20, **26sts**)
Row 5. * K2 tog; repeat from * to end. (8, **9**, 10, **13sts**)
Row 7. * K2 tog; repeat from * to end, ending K-, (**1**, - , **1**).
(4, **5**, 5, **7sts**)
Break off yarn and thread through the remaining sts. Fasten off.

Make up:
Fold hem under at picot edge and sew. Stitch back from crown for 2 (**2.5**, 4, **5**)cm. Sew on ribbons.

BOOTEES

Cast on 16 (**18**, 22, **24**)sts and work first 6 rows as for dress.

51cm size only: Work 4 rows in stocking st.

All sizes:

Next row. (Ribbon holes) * K1, yfwd, K2 tog; repeat from * to end.

Next row. Purl.

Next row. K10 (**12**, 14, **16**)sts, turn.

Next row. P4 (**6**, 6, **8**)sts, turn.

Work 2 (**2**, 4, **6**) rows on these sts. Break off yarn.

Rejoin yarn and with right side facing, pick up 1 (**2**, 3, **4**)sts up the first side of instep, K4 (**6**, 6, **8**)sts of instep and the pick up and K1 (**2**, 3, **4**)sts down the other side of instep. Knit sts from left-hand needle. (18, **22**, 28, **32sts**)

Next and alternate rows. Purl.

Next row. K2 tog, K5 (**7**, 9, **11**), K2 tog, K- (-, 2, **2**), K2 tog, K5 (**7**, 9, **11**), K2 tog. (14, **18**, 24, **28sts**)

Next row. K2 tog, K3 (**5**, 7, **9**), K2 tog, K- (-, 2, **2**), K2 tog, K3 (**5**, 7, **9**), K2 tog. (10, **14**, 20, **24sts**)

Next row. K2 tog, K1 (**3**, 5, **7**), K2 tog, K- (-, 2, **2**), K2 tog, K1 (**3**, 5, **7**), K2 tog. (6, **10**, 16, **20sts**)

Cast off.

Work a second bootee the same.

Make up:

Turn hem to row of holes onto wrong side and sew. Join the leg and base of foot of each bootee. Thread ribbon through the ribbon-holes.

LITTLE GIRL DOLL

To fit doll sizes:
35cm (40cm) in height

Chest: 16.5cm (20.25cm)

MATERIALS:
Skirt, Jumper, Jacket, Hat:
4 (5) 25g balls red 8ply yarn
1 (1) 25g ball white 8ply yarn
5 small buttons for jumper
40cm elastic
piece of cardboard for pom-pom

Vest, Dress, Panties:
1 (1) 25g ball of white 8ply yarn
3 (3) 25g balls of blue 8ply yarn
1 (1) 25g ball of red 8ply yarn
2 small buttons
25cm elastic for panties

SKIRT

SKIRT BACK and FRONT (Alike)
Using red, cast on 48 (54)sts.
Row 1. * K4, P2; repeat from * to end.
Row 2. * K2, P4; repeat from * to end.
Repeat these 2 rows until work measures 5 (6.5)cm, ending with a row 2.
Next row. * K1, K2 tog, K1, P2; repeat from * to end. (40, 45sts)
Next row. * K2, P3; repeat from * to end.
Work 4 more rows in rib without shaping.

Next row. * K2 tog, K1, P2; repeat from * to end. (32, 36sts)
Next row. * K2, P2; repeat from * to end.
Next row. K1, * yfwd, K2 tog; repeat from * to last st, K1.
Next row. * K2, P2; repeat from * to end. Cast off.

Work second side to correspond.

Make up:
Stitch up side seams and thread elastic through holes at waist.

JUMPER

JUMPER FRONT
Using white, cast on 20 (22)sts and work 3 rows in stocking st.
Row 4. (Wrong side facing) Knit.
Row 5. * Knit in white.
Row 6. Purl in white.
Repeat last 2 rows once.
Join in red yarn, carrying colour not in use up side of work.
Rows 9 and 10. Using red knit. **

Repeat in white and red stripes from * to ** 4 (4) times more, break off red.

Using white, work 3 more rows in stocking st. Cast off.

JUMPER BACK
Work as for front for first 8 rows.
Row 9. Join in red and K10 (11)sts, turn.
Row 10. Working on these sts, knit to end.
Continue in stripes until the work measures same length as front. Cast off.

Join red and white to centre of remaining sts and work second side to correspond. Cast off.

Make up:
Stitch up shoulder seams for 2.5cm and side seams as far as 3rd (2nd) red stripe. Turn up hem on wrong side along the purl row and sew loosely.

Using white, work a row of double crochet down right back edge working a 5 chain loop at top, and in the centre of each white band until 5 loops in all have been made.

Continue in double crochet up opposite side of opening and round neck. Crochet around the armholes. Stitch on buttons to correspond with loops.

JACKET

JACKET BACK
Using red, cast on 26 (28)sts, and work 3 rows in stocking st.

Row 4. (Wrong side facing) Knit.

Row 5. Knit.

Row 6. Purl.

Repeat last 2 rows 5 (6) times more, then cast off 2sts at the beginning of the next 2 rows (for armhole). Continue until work measures 12 (12.5)cm from beginning. Cast off.

JACKET LEFT FRONT
Using red, cast on 9 (11)sts and work as for back until the first 4 rows have been worked.

Row 5. Knit.

Row 6. K3, purl to end.

Repeat last 2 rows 5 (6) times more then cast off 2sts at beginning of next row.

Continue to repeat rows 5 and 6 until work measures 11.5 (12)cm from beginning, ending with row 5.

Next row. Cast off 3sts, purl to end.

Next row. Knit to last 2sts, K2 tog. Cast off.

JACKET RIGHT FRONT
Work as for left front until 5 rows have been worked.

Row 6. Purl to last 3sts, K3.

Row 7. Knit.

Complete as for left front, reversing armhole and neck shaping.

Cast off.

JACKET SLEEVES (make 2)
Using red, cast on 16 (18)sts and work the first 6 rows as for back of jacket.

Continue in stocking st, increase one st at each end of next row and every following 3rd row until there are 26 (28)sts on the needle.

Work another 6 (8) rows without shaping. Cast off.

Make up:
Sew up shoulder and side seams to armholes. Sew up sleeves and stitch into armholes. Sew up hems on cuffs and round lower edge of jacket as for base of *jumper*.

HAT
Using red, cast on 45 (50)sts. Work first 6 rows as for back of *jacket*, then rows 5 and 6 again. Join on white and repeat from * to ** of *jumper* 3 times.

Decrease as follows in white:

Row 1. * K5, K2 tog; repeat from * to last 3 (1)sts, K3 (1). (39, 43sts)

Row 2 and alternate rows. Purl.

Row 3. * K4, K2 tog; repeat from * to last 3 (1)sts, K3 (1). (33, 36sts)

Row 5. Using red, * K3, K2 tog; repeat from * to the last 3 (1)sts, K3 (1). (27, 29sts)

Still working in stripes continue to decrease in a similar manner until 9 (8)sts remain.

Row 12. Knit.

Break off yarn and thread through remaining stitches, fastening off securely.

Make up:
Turn up hem to wrong side and sew. Sew up side of hat. Cut 2 circles of cardboard 4.5cm in diameter, each with a hole 1.5cm in diameter in the centre. Wind yarn round both pieces of cardboard fairly firmly until the hole is completely filled up. Cut around edge between the 2 pieces of cardboard and tie firmly in centre with double yarn, leaving sufficient to stitch pom-pom to top of hat. Trim to spherical shape.

VEST

Using white, cast on 18 (22)sts and work in rib as follows:

Row 1. * K2, P2; repeat from * to last 2sts, K2.

Row 2. * P2, K2; repeat from * to last 2sts, P2.

Repeat these 2 rows until work measures 8 (9.5)cm from the beginning.

Next row. Rib 5 (6)sts, cast off 8 (10)sts, rib to end.

Next row. Work 12 (14) rows on this last set of 5 (6)sts, ending at inside edge. Break off yarn.

Rejoin yarn to the second group of sts, and work 12 (14) rows, ending at inside edge. Cast on 8 (10)sts and work across remaining group of sts. Continue in rib for 7 (8.5)cm. Cast off in rib.

Make up:

Fold over into half and stitch up side seams, leaving enough opening for armholes.

DRESS
(Very small waisted)
DRESS FRONT

Using blue, cast on 47 (53)sts and work 3 rows in moss st.

Row 4. Purl, increase one st at end of row. 48 (54)sts.

Row 5. * K2 tog, K12 (14), K2 tog through back of loop; repeat from * to end. (42, 48sts)

Work 3 rows in stocking st.

Row 9. * K2 tog, K10 (12), K2 tog through back of loop; repeat from * to end. (36, 42sts)
Repeat last 4 rows, continuing to decrease in this way, knitting 2sts less between the decrease sts until 12 (18)sts remain.
Work 1 (3) more rows in stocking st without shaping.
Next row. K3 (5), increase in next st, K4 (6), increase in next st, K3 (5). (14, 20sts)
Next row. Purl.
Next row. K3 (5), increase in next st, K6 (8), increase in next st, K3 (5). (16, 22sts)
Next row. Purl.
Next row. K3 (5), increase in next st, K8 (10), increase in next st, K3 (5). (18, 24sts)
Next row. Purl.
Next row. Cast on 3 (3)sts, knit to end. (21, 27sts)
Next row. Cast on 3 (3)sts, purl to last 2sts, K2. (24, 30sts)
Work 10 (12) rows in stocking st without shaping, keeping the 2sts at each end in garter st for the sleeves.

Neck shaping:
K8 (10), cast off 8 (10)sts, K8 (10).
Work 2 rows in stocking st on these last 8 (10)sts.
Next row. Cast off 4 (5)sts, purl to end. (4, 5sts)
Next row. Knit.

Cast off the remaining sts.

Join yarn to other side and work to correspond. Cast off.

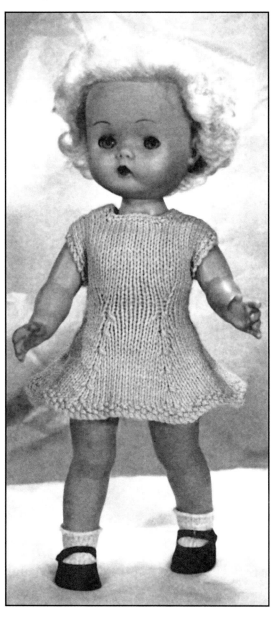

DRESS BACK

Work as for front until the purl row following the waist increases has been completed. (18, 24sts)

Next row. Cast on 3 (3)sts, K12 (15), turn.

Next row. K2, P8 (11), K2.

Next row. Knit.

Repeat last 2 rows 5 (6) times.

Next row. Cast off 4 (5)sts, P6 (8), K2.

Work 2 rows on these 8 (10)sts, keeping the garter st border at the sleeve edge.

Next row. Cast off 4 (5)sts, knit to end.

Next row. Purl.

Cast off the remaining sts.

Join yarn to other side and work to correspond.

Make up:

Stitch up side and shoulder seams. Work a row of double crochet around neck and finish off back opening with 2 button loops as for back of jumper (see page 13). Stitch on buttons to correspond with loops.

PANTIES

Using red or blue (to match either skirt or dress), cast on 18 (20)sts and work in (K1, P1) rib for 2 rows.

Next row. (Make elastic holes) K1, * K1, yfwd, K2 tog; repeat from * to last 2 (1)sts, K2 (1).

Next row. Rib.

Work 6 rows in stocking st.

To shape legs:

K2 tog at each end of every row until 6sts remain.

Work on these sts for 7 (9) rows.

Increase one st at each end of every row until there are 18 (20)sts on needle.

Work 7 rows in stocking st.

Next row. Rib.

Next row. (Make elastic holes) K1, * K1, yfwd, K2 tog; repeat from * to last 2 (1)sts, K2 (1).

Rib 2 rows. Cast off.

Make up:

Join side seams. Thread elastic through holes at waist.

TEENAGE DOLL

To fit doll 25cm in height

MATERIALS:

Sweater and Slacks:
1 (25g) ball turquoise 8ply yarn
1 (25g) ball navy blue 8ply yarn
3 buttons

Skating outfit:
Skirt, Jumper, Beanie and Briefs:
1 (25g) ball gold 8ply yarn
1 (25g) ball white 8ply yarn
oddment navy blue 8ply yarn
2 small buttons.

Cape and Hat:
1 (25g) ball olive green 8ply yarn

Dress:
1 (25g) ball turquoise 8ply yarn

SWEATER

SWEATER FRONT
Using turquoise, cast on 14sts and work 2 rows in garter st (hem).
Change to stocking st and work border as follows:
Row 3. Join in navy, * K2 turquoise, K2 navy; repeat from * to last 2sts, K2 turquoise.
Row 4. * P2 navy, P2 turquoise; repeat from * to last 2sts, P2 navy.
Row 5. * K2 turquoise, K2 navy; repeat from * to last 2sts, K2 turquoise. Break off navy.

Row 6. Using turquoise, purl to end.
Work 3cm in stocking st, ending with a purl row.

Cast on 2sts at the beginning of each of the next 4 rows and then 6sts at the beginning of the following 2 rows, ending last row K2. (34sts)
Next row. Knit.
Next row. K2, P30, K2.
Repeat last 2 rows once.

Cast off 6sts at the beginning of each of the next 2 rows.
Next row. Cast off 5sts, rib 12sts (K1, P1 rib), K5.
Next row. Cast off 5sts, rib 12sts.

Work 4 more rows of rib on remaining 12sts. Cast off in rib.

SWEATER RIGHT BACK
Using turquoise, cast on 7sts and work 2 rows in garter st (hem).
Row 3. Join in navy, K2 turquoise, K2 navy, K2 turquoise, K1 navy.
Row 4. P1 turquoise, P2 navy, P2 turquoise, P2 navy.
Row 5. K2 turquoise, K2 navy, K2 turquoise, K1 navy. Break off navy.
Row 6. Using turquoise, purl to end.
Work 3cm in stocking st, ending with a purl row.

Cast on 2sts at the beginning of the next 2 alternate rows.
Next row. Purl.
Next row. Cast on 6sts, knit to end. (17sts)
Next row. Purl to last 2sts, K2.

Work 4 more rows, knitting the last 2sts at end of each purl row.
Next row. Cast off 6sts, knit to end.
Next row. Purl.
Next row. Cast off 5sts, rib (K1, P1) to end.

Work 5 rows in rib on remaining 6sts. Cast off in rib.

SWEATER LEFT BACK
Cast on 7sts and work to correspond with right back, reversing sleeve shapings.
Cast off in rib.

Make up:
Stitch up side and sleeve seams, top of sleeves and polo neck. Turn up hem at lower edge and sew. Turn over collar to right side and sew down. Work a row of double crochet down right hand back making a chain loop at top, middle and bottom for buttons. Sew on buttons.

SLACKS

SLACKS RIGHT LEG
** Using navy, cast on 10sts, and work 2 rows in garter st (hem).

Join in turquoise and work as follows:

Row 3. (K2 turquoise, K2 navy) twice, K2 turquoise.
Row 4. (P2 navy, P2 turquoise) twice, P2 navy.
Row 5. (K2 turquoise, K2 navy) twice, K2 turquoise. Break off turquoise.

Continue in navy working 10 rows in stocking st, then increase one st at each end of next row and every following third row until there are 16sts on the needle. Continue without shaping for a further 12 rows. **

Back shaping:
(With wrong side facing) P4, turn.
Row 2. Knit back.

Row 3. P8, turn.
Row 4. Knit back.
Row 5. P12, turn.
Row 6. Knit back.
Row 7. Purl right across.
Work 3 rows in K1, P1 rib.
Cast off.

SLACKS LEFT LEG
Work as for right leg from ** to **.
Next row. Purl.

Back shaping:
(Right side facing) K4, turn.
Row 2. Purl back.
Row 3. K8, turn.
Row 4. Purl back.
Row 5. K12, turn.
Row 6. Purl back.
Row 7. Knit right across.
Work 3 rows in K1, P1 rib.
Cast off.

Make up:
Turn up hems at lower edges. Stitch up inside leg seams, then front and back seams.

SKATING OUTFIT

SKATING SKIRT

Using gold, cast on 20sts (waist) and work 3 rows in garter st.

Row 4. K2, * yfwd, K1, yfwd, K4; repeat from * to last 3sts, yfwd, K1, yfwd, K2.

Row 5 and every alternate row. Purl.

Row 6. K3, * yfwd, K1, yfwd, K6; repeat from * to last 4sts, yfwd, K1, yfwd, K3.

Continue in this manner, increasing 8sts on every other row until there are 68sts on the needles.

Cast off purlwise.

Make up:
Stitch up back seam. Using navy, work a row of double crochet around lower edge.

SKATING JUMPER

Using white, cast on 12sts and work 6 rows in stocking st.

Next row. K3, increase in next st, K4, increase in next st, K3.

Next row. Purl.

Cast off one st at the beginning of each of the next 2 rows.

Work 4 rows in stocking st.

Next row. K4, cast off 4sts, K4.

Work 7 rows on this last set of 4sts, then cast on 2sts.

Work 5 rows in stocking st.

Next row. Cast on one stitch, purl to end.

Next row. Knit.

Next row. P3, P2 tog, P2.

Work 6 rows in stocking st.
Cast off. Break off yarn.

Rejoin yarn to inside edge of remaining sts, purl to end.
Work 5 more rows in stocking st without shaping.
Next row. Cast on 2sts, purl to end.
Work 4 more rows in stocking st without shaping.
Next row. Cast on one stitch, knit to end.
Next row. Purl.
Next row. K3, K2 tog, K2.
Work 6 rows in stocking st.
Cast off.

SLEEVES (make 2)
Using white, cast on 8sts and work in stocking st for 14 rows.
Next row. Increase one stitch at each end of row.
Next row. Purl.

Shape armholes:
Cast off one stitch at the beginning of each of the next 2 rows. Work 2 more rows in stocking st. Cast off remaining sts.

Make up:
Stitch up side seams. Using navy, work a row of double crochet around cuffs. Stitch up sleeve seams and sew into armholes. With right side facing, join navy yarn at hem and work a row of double crochet up left back opening, around neck and down right back opening, making a small chain loop at top of right side and another three quarters of the way down. Using white, work a row of double crochet round lower edge of jumper to prevent edge curling up. Stitch on buttons to correspond with crochet loops.

SKATING BEANIE
Using navy, cast on 30sts, and work 3 rows in garter st.
Join in gold (carry colour not in use up side of work) and work 4 rows in stocking st, then using navy work 2 rows in garter st.
Join in white and work 4 rows in stocking st.
Using navy knit 2 rows.
Using gold, work 4 rows in stocking stitch.

Next row. Using navy, * K3, K2 tog; repeat from * to end. (24sts)
Next row. Knit.
Using white, work 4 rows in stocking st.
Next row. Using navy, * K2, K2 tog; repeat from * to end. (18sts)
Next row. Knit
Work 4 rows in gold.
Next row. Using navy, * K1, K2 tog; repeat from * to end. (12sts)

Next row. Knit.
Work 4 rows in white.
Next row. Using navy, * K2 tog; repeat from * to end. (6sts)
Next row. Knit.
Break off yarn, thread through remaining 6sts and fasten off firmly.

Make up:
Stitch up seam. Make a tassel in gold and attach to point of beanie. Fold over point and catch down.

BRIEFS

Using either navy (for skating outfit) or olive green (for dress), cast on 13sts and work 2 rows in K1, P1 rib. Change to stocking st and work 6 rows.
K2 tog at each end of every row until 3sts remain.
Work 3 rows in stocking st.

Increase one stitch at each end of every row until there are 13sts on the needle.
Work 6 rows in stocking st.
Work 2 rows in K1, P1 rib.
Cast off.

Make up:
Stitch up side seams.

CAPE

Using olive green, cast on 14sts (neck edge).
Row 1. K4, increase 1 (by picking up the loop at base of next st on left-hand needle and knitting into it), K1, increase 1, K4, increase 1, K1, increase 1, K4.
Row 2 and every alternate row. K2, purl to last 2sts, K2.
Row 3. K5, increase 1 (as before), K1, increase 1, K6, increase 1, K1, increase 1, K5.
Continue in this way, increasing 4sts on every other row until there are 46sts on the needle.

Row 17. K9 (slip these sts onto a safety pin), K3, increase 1, K1, increase 1, K20, increase 1, K1, increase 1, P3, (slip remaining sts onto second safety pin).
Row 18 and alternate rows. K2, purl to last 2sts, K2.
Row 19. K4, increase 1, K1, increase 1, K22, increase 1, K1, increase 1, K4. (36sts)
Row 21. Knit.
Row 22. K2, purl to last 2sts, K2.
Repeat last 2 rows twice more.

With right side facing, slip 9sts from safety pin onto the needle, rejoin yarn and work 8 rows in stocking st on these 9sts, keeping the 2sts at each end in garter st.

Next row. Knit. Break off yarn.

Slip the remaining sts onto a needle and work 8 rows on these to match first strip, ending with a purl row - working last 2sts, K2.

Work 8 rows in stocking st on these 54sts, keeping the 2 edge sts in garter st, and knitting 2sts tog at the end of the last row. (53sts)

Change to moss st, and work 6 rows. Cast off.

Make up:
Crochet 2 chains 12.5cm long and attach to each front at neck edge, knot the ends. Use chains to tie under chin.

HAT

Using olive green, cast on 7sts and work 13.5cm in moss st. Cast off. Join into a ring. This forms the band.

HAT CROWN

Using crochet hook, make 5 chain and join with a slip st to form a ring.

Work 3 rows of double crochet round this, working twice into each st on the second and third rounds. Fasten off and stitch crown inside hat band.

DRESS

DRESS FRONT

Using turquoise, cast on 29sts and work 7 rows in moss st.

Next row. P2 tog across row to last st, K1.

Proceed in stocking st until work measures 9cm from the beginning.

Change to moss st and work 6 rows.

Next row. Moss st 5sts, cast off 5sts for neck, moss st to end.

Work 6 rows in moss st on last 5sts. Cast off.

Rejoin yarn to remaining 5sts and work to correspond. Cast off.

DRESS BACK

Cast on 29sts and work as for front. Cast off.

Make up:

Stitch up side seams to beginning of moss st yoke, then shoulder seams.

The following Paragon knitting books are also available

These books are also available (by Vicki Moodie, unless shown otherwise)

BK02	Hooked on Lace
BK03	Needles and Lace
BK04	Top that Towel
BK05	Laced with Love
BK06	More Towel Tops
BK07	Novelties in Lace
BK08	Paragon of Lace
BK09	Keep it Cosy
BK10	Basics in Lace
BK11	Knitted Coat-hanger Covers
BK12	Towel Tops & Motifs
BK13	Simple Jug Covers
BK14	More Knitted Lace
BK15	Easy Crocheted Bootees
BK16	Kitchen Towels
BK17	Doilies for my Daughter
BK18	Baby's Crocheted Rugs and Shawls
BK19	Crocheted Matinee Jackets
BK20	Baby's Knitted Rugs and Shawls
BK21	More Jug Covers
BK22	Crocheted Three Piece Sets
BK23	Occasional Lace
BK24	Crocheted Outfits for Dolls and Prem Babies
BK25	Doilies to crochet in 4ply cotton
BK26	Knitted Outfits for Dolls and Prem Babies (by Denny Kelly)
BK27	More Knitted Outfits for Dolls and Prem Babies
BK28	A Crocheted Library of Bookmarks
BK29	Hairpin Crochet Made Easy (by Betty Franks)
BK30	Animal Towel Tops and More
BK31	Favourite Knitted Outfits for Dolls and Prems
BK32	Showtime Tea Cosies
BK33	Crocheted Novelty Dressing Table Sets
BK34 (A4)	Crocheted Baby Shawls Round and Rectangle
BK35 (A4)	More Crocheted Shawls for Baby
BK36 (A4)	Crocheted Bags for Beginners
BK37 (A4)	Crocheted Coathanger Covers Book 1
BK38 (A4)	Stylish Jug Covers
BK39 (A4)	Distinctive Jug Covers to Crochet
BK40 (A4)	Crocheted Baby Outfits - Newborn to 9 months
BK41 (A4)	Dream Catchers and More to Crochet
BK42 (A4)	Four More Crocheted Dressing Table Sets
BK43 (A4)	Crocheted Doilies using Broomstick, Bavarian & Daisy Wheel
BK44 (A4)	Inspirational Tea Cosies knitted and crocheted
BKAG01	Sculptured Candlewicking (by Anne Green)
BKAG02	Australiana Candlewicking (by Anne Green)